THE POWER OF SEXUALITY

WORKBOOK

OPEN YOURSELF TO LOVE

Zhannet M.S., Juliia U.L.

ISBN:

2

Table of Contents

Foreword of Julia

Hello dear. If you are holding this book in your hands, then most likely, the time has come for your global transformation, and the Universe has sent you as a gift one of the most powerful tools for working on oneself. "Work on Oneself" in the context of this book involves the disclosure of one's sexuality (getting pleasure from all processes in life) in all its possible completeness, raising the energy of true femininity, lifting the ban on pleasure, allowing yourself to finally be yourself and accepting yourself beloved in all its manifestations. Women are light, is divine, being composed with 100% love, from the love that she brings into her life every moment of their wonderful life. This love in its diverse manifestations is in each of us, it is a Divine spirit, it is a gift of love from the great Universe, this love begins with self-love. The way of healing oneself consists of love and acceptance of oneself.To love and accept the versatility of your personality with its shadow manifestations, resource, and non-resource sides, to begin with, these need to be discovered within yourself.

There are practices and technical books created to help on this segment of your large-scale and exciting transformational journey..

Once the wisest, my favorite and the Divine essence, significant for me, to the question "what should I do next" answered me "love" !!!

Just in love .... "in the sense of ...." I thought ... "all living things need love, plants, animals, people, everything that you touch, everything that you interact with, everything that is in your presence every day, it all needs love. And when you realize that love is the greatest value for all living things, you begin to do what you can with the maximum expression of love. "she answered me. One of the greatest knowledge of my life consists of one word," love". When you do what an expression of your love to the world is, it is essentially going along the path that corresponds to the ideal Divine and Universal plan created for us.This harmony with yourself and with the surrounding space of practice and technology books that pave your way to you, the way you find answers to your questions, and all the important and necessary information for you. Book tools help you hear yourself, listen to yourself and trust yourself.

"Do good in all the earth, do good to others for the good", is my main mantra of love in my life. Over the years of practice, thousands of hours of work on myself having gone with leaps and bounds, my path of transformation for the next decade, I realized I describe the spiritual practice of "living life with love and benefit to the world." The main spiritual practice in a relationship, loved ones, with parents, with friends, with neighbors, in relationships with everyone around us. The main spiritual practice is the concentration on the object + gratuitous service to him. Full concentration on the person with whom we communicate, maybe even 15 minutes, but wholly devoted to that person. Do not be distracted by the phone, do not think about work, but listen and hear who is nearby. When we listen and hear the one nearby, we understand what a person truly needs, how we can be useful to them, how we can help them, what we can make for them, and from this realization comes gratuitous service with love. Gratuitous service with love is possible through the understanding that we are one, soul mates only born in another place, in another family, at another time, and other environmental factors. Every day I ask myself, "what am I bringing to the world today." Every evening before going to bed, I ask myself " what did I do today to make the world easier from my existence.Life is a gift! The biggest.

Its value lies in the fact that life in this physical world makes it possible for our soul to develop and transform. In our time, in our world there are all the instruments contributing to the development of our personality for the benefit of all living creatures, and every hit on the keyboard keys creates another such instruction.

I try as much as possible and put all my knowledge and skills into the creation of this book and thank The Universe for this opportunity to express to the world the awareness and signs, skills, and experience. I know that it will be created for the good, because if it exists in it, just as in everything in this world there is a particle of God if it is created, then the creator needs it in this world, at this ideal moment in time.

With LOVE !!!
Juliia U.L.

Foreword of Jeannette

Greetings, dear reader! My name is Jeannette M.S. The book you hold in your hands is a logical continuation of my author's transformational games, "Mantra of sexuality." Together with the talented Julia, the host of this game, we created a practical book, a stimulating book, and a weekly book for developing sexuality. No matter how you call this work, the essence is the same - the book is not intended for educational reading, but for internal work on yourself.

The game lasts only a few hours, leaving behind a new experience and task. The third round of the game closes the participants in action - a particular step, to be done in reality. One woman immediately decide on it; the other waits a long time.

This book is sure to help consolidate and develop the result of the game. All practices proposed here pursue a single goal - to create new sensations and experiences, skills in the development of their sexuality. The book can also be used independently as a personal guide to self-study and a guide to help you become more aware of your topic of sexuality.

I am especially inspired by the beneficial effect of the game on relationships in a married couple - this is the most crucial and challenging part of our efforts. According to

Scandinavian scholars Kjell Nordstrom and Jonas Ridderstrale in the book "Funky Business," our entire civilization is moving towards different forms of social loneliness. There are predictions that after 30 years, people will mainly live alone, locked in small apartments. Recognizing the Impossibility to influence this global trend, I nevertheless strive to make every effort to preserve and maintain family values.

In preparing this publication, we combined experience and practice, individual best practices, vision, awareness - in this way, each reader can find something in tune with yourself. This book is also support for each other, a warm circle of interesting women. Together, it's easier for us to promote a global idea, a goal for which games, books, and training work: enhancing the sexual intelligence of society.

By the sexual intelligence of a woman, we mean the internal permission to be happy, contented, active, and holistic. Able to realize their personal values - create a family, become a mother, enjoy anything, not just sexual interaction. She understands where her desires are and where imposed, and what exactly is her personal truth.

That is why, in this topic, there is a place for everything, even the most exalted and the most mundane. There is no place for condemnation and taboos.

Every woman is free to make a decision on how to deal with your body, and no one has the right to condemn it. Whatever happens in her life is just a topic for research. Unfortunately,we often hear some things we desire in bed are wrong. Courage, frankness, honesty, and faith in the reproductive potential of every woman, shown by the authors of this book, by themselves, are capable of changing something in the reader's inner landscape.

Real sexuality is not only about sex, but it is also about the quality of being in contact and pleasure. Everyone can primitively copulate, but fo to truly enjoy sexuality, you need to give yourself permission to enjoy,be honest, and deep interaction. Opposing the excessive dramatization of events and relationships, we recognize the value of a variety of experiences - they can all be about the fullness of life, about sexuality and revelation.

Do not forget that you have already been born a woman. Everything that you need for the manifestation of sexuality is already inside, in the development of sexuality.

Intelligence is a simple task: to take small, feasible, and sincere steps towards yourself. Since this book is interesting to you, it means that you already have a lot of manifested sexual energy, and the impulse to open it further is quite strong.

And one more important point that I would like to draw your attention too. Internal work, self-knowledge sometimes takes a lot of time - but equally, you have to realize your sexuality in contact with others. It is no coincidence that tasks for men will soon appear in the game, and they can become its full participants. So they will learn to understand what the woman is talking about and what she is silent about. After all, the main task of the game is to provoke dialogue, honest, and beautiful interaction between a man and a woman. And there soon a new book will be written ... for men.

P.S. "Sexuality is a bait for absorption" - this is the only quote of my authorship that is used in the game. You know, I haven't told anyone about it yet. "

With LOVE !!!
Zhannet M.S.

Archetype of Mary

The archetype of Mary is the archetype of spirituality. This archetype reveals the high meanings of being, is responsible for the skill of unconditional love. Mary's archetype reveals a heart for unconditional love. The energy boost of manyarchetype for every woman is healing.

Mary's archetype helps to understand how the energy of life flows in our body and how we can help ourselves on the energetic plane and improve our lives when we gain knowledge in this area. The archetype of Mary teaches us acceptance. Not just agree with something, but truly accept the nature of things as they are. Mary's religious beliefs help a person to take awkward moments of life. Mary's archetype teaches us the highest meanings of life, appropriate austerities, and respect for our divine essence.

Archetype of Eve

The Eve archetype symbolizes and carries through itself the energy of the wife and mother. Wife, who respects her husband, faithful, beautiful, keeper of the earth, mother and women who can get pregnant, bear and give birth to healthy children. The strong side of Eve's archetype is love and service.

Understanding that home is the earth and like a mother's bosom, understanding the importance of home, home comfort, and the fact that only she can create such conditions. Archetype Eva reveals the ability to create her own hands and to reveal the beauty of her body in a feminine way. Eve is love; it is the feeling that we must to teach our children. Only by transmitting love into the world can a woman be creative. The answer to all life questions and situations is love. Love, and take every step of your life through love, and then you will undoubtedly advance through life in accordance with the divine plan for you.

Archetype of Sophia

The main purpose of the archetype of Sofia is to help a woman know herself, to know her female nature in terms of how to realize herself socially. To know yourself, answer the questions "who am I," what do I want, to realize my true desires and needs. Sophia is wisdom, this is intelligence, this is the woman's social status in society, it's about how a woman sees herself, her talents, that help her make money. Sofia shows that a woman who knows herself realizes the needs of other people, she knows how to feel, she knows how to think strategically, she is wise, her intellect is very high, especially in the area of oneself. The archetype of Sophia helps to realize and focus on the physiological needs of your body. Archetype of Sofia also teaches with every problem to see the possibilities.

Archetype of Lilith

The Archetype of Lilith characterizes an insanely beautiful, sexy, attractive women, a woman who can realize any sexual dreams and fantasies, Lilith women is a woman who herself knows how to get the most out of life. Lilith is a woman who worships a man who is not trying to redo it and admires the way he is.

Archetype Lilith speaks about passion, about pleasure, about being a rebel in a cool way, teaches perception the process of sex for pleasure, but only for the sake of having children. Lilith archetype promotes pleasures for your body too.

IMPORTANCE OF NUTRITIONS

The Importance of Nutrition is hard to overestimate in our ever-evolving world. In the world of beauty, health, achievements, in the process of continually increasing energy and vibrations of humans and their surroundings, eating food daily, enjoying its taste, it's appearance, learning the features of different gastronomic cuisines of the world.Most people, based on our pictures of the world rarely think about what food is medicine for the body and soul that we use daily. A conscious attitude to food is an excellent tool for development in various areas of our lives. With food, we can effectively increase the vibration of its energy and subtle bodies, grounding as needed, activation of sexual energy, improved concentration and brain, activity, cleansing the body, and natural pleasure. Pleasuresare one of the highest divine gifts to humanity.

Pleasure

____

____

MARY. BODY. DIET

The diet that helps cleanse the subtle and energetic bodies of a person. Thanks to the products of this diet, energy vibrations increase, which subsequently leads to increased communication with the Divine.

A WEEKLY DIET FOR ARCHETYPE "MARY BODY"

Add products of the following categories to the diet:		Remove products of the following categories from the diet:	
Day of water (we recommend making it regular weekly practice on Mondays)		roots (for grounding energy)	
Fruits (raw, pure, smoothie, fresh juice)		cofe	

Vegetables (raw, pure, smoothie, fresh juice)		meat	
Chia seeds		fish	
		grains	
		onion	

RECOMMENDATIONS FOR PRACTICE OF WEEKLY POST AND ABSTAIN FROM FOOD ON MONDAY.

Abstinence from food on this day of the week is recommended for almost everyone (if there are no constraints from a doctor), since it evens out the general emotional background. Improves living conditions, including by solving lingering problems. The body joyfully responds to such a radical solution that day. By supporting this practice every week, a person noticeably heals. There is a high probability of establishing relationships in the family especially with p

MARY. BODY.SPIRITUALITY.ASCETICISM

Often going into spiritual practice or other life flows, we forget about the needs of the body. What have you forgotten about? What are you doing for your body?.

ASSIGNMENT: describe the 10 needs of your body. When will you satisfy them? How will this affect the decision of your request?

1.____

2.____

3.____

4.____

5.____

6.____

7.____

8.____

9.____

10.____

FEMALE SEXUALITY is a "complex of qualities in one person. When there are healthy irony and sarcasm in relation to everything around, with outward smiling and gracious a sense of humor and wit.

MARY.BODY. SPIRITUAL PRACTICE

A powerful technique for cleansing the subtle body and emotional plane is a daily morning bath. It cleanses at the level of the subtle body, including after night, ablution after a working day. We recommend using salt as a body scrub or bath additive. Salt is a strong absorbent of negative energy and subtle human bodies.

After cleansing, we recommend doing the practice for your body and with love, energy, and space around you.

Sit for 10 minutes in silence, lower the focus of attention into yourself, observe your breathing, feel the temperature of the space with your body, the touch. Listen to the sounds in the area around you say out loud or mentally "I wish everyone happiness," "I wish everyone Divine love" - and imagine how the energy of bliss and love pervades every cell and living beings. Primarily to your offenders.

FOR THE BENEFIT

MARY.EMOTION.WEEKLY. DIET

The goal of the recommendations of this diet is to achieve a harmonious emotional zen state. The product of this diet will help you to achieve emotional balance, contributes to a stronger connection with your inner self, and the elective manifestation of the necessary answers to existing questions.

Add products of the following categories to the diet:		Remove products of the following categories from the diet:	
Water day (all day just drinking water)		Meat	
Dry fruits		Fish	
Berries		Red fruits	
Vegetables and herbs pure		Red vegetables	
Chopped herbs with oil as sauces		Bread	

Grains		Onion	
Chia seeds		Garlick	

RECOMMENDATIONS FOR THE USE OF CHIA SEEDS.

Useful properties and application. Chia seeds are an excellent means for weight loss. Omega 3 contains 8 times more than the same amount contained in 100g salmon or walnuts. High calcium content is included in the seeds. Chia seeds lower blood sugar, prevent constipation, support the nervous system and heart. It is recommended to drink chia seeds with milk or juice, adding fruit or vegetable salads.
WITH LOVE

MARY. EMOTIONS.SPIRITUALITY. ASCETICISM

For women, it is very important to recognize the aspect of the offender and begin to work with him. When you feel discontent and rejection of sexuality in yourself, remember that the more discontent and anger you feel, the more you associate yourself with the victim's role and the more freedom you take away from yourself.

Forgive yourself, and you will forgive others. Write a letter of forgiveness.

FEMALE SEXUALITY varies depending on the setting and environment. From the man who is nearby.

MARY.EMOTIONS. SPIRITUALITY. ASCETICISM

MEDITATION FOR CLEANING THE INTERIOR AND THE ENVIRONMENT

Take a comfortable body rise, relax as much as possible, focus on your breathing. Gather the entire focus of attention to one point inside your physical body.

Transform the entire clot of your attention into an object that is maximally effective to cleanse your inner space (sponge, mop, rag, maybe your unconsciously creative for so much that will offer an option unexpected for you. Trust and follow your unconscious). Now imagine where inside you in a visual form of dirt such conditions as anger, fears, anger his resentment, sadness, negativity, disappointment ....

Now using your magical item of purity, begin spring cleaning inside you fun and with pleasure. Sweep, wash, and destroy all the dirt inside. Throw it into outer space.

After the cleaning inside is over, imagine all the same non-resource states in the space around you like all the same dirt. Focus of attention, and he will transfer the magical object of purification from the inner space to the outer one and begin to clean the space just as carefully. Further, we throw this garbage outside and, under the scheme described above, clear the space mentally collecting all the garbage and throw it away.

Further, for example, to a map of the city (a visual image of the city), then according to the same scheme to the level of a clean country, then to the space of the Universe in which there is no divisions and duality, in which there is no limit.

We imagine how, under the ray of Divine light, all the dirt and the object of creating purity are converted into pure life-giving energy in the form of a golden glow or golden sparkling dust. This golden glow or dust particles are beautifully dispersed and dissolved in the boundless expanses of the space of the universe.

Take three deep breaths through the solar plexus zone and open your eyes.

Thank yourself for the work, the Universe, for the work; thank your unconscious for work.

FOR THE BENEFIT

MARY.CONVICTIONS.SPIRITUAL ITY.ASCETICISM. TECHNIQUE

Reasons for women's dissatisfaction and enjoyment depend on social and moral charters. Like everything with humans, it does not rely only on nature. If there is a desire, it must be filled and "enjoyed." Which shades set's your enjoyment? What do they protect you from?

SHADE:do you recognize the consequences of dissatisfaction?

____

____

____

____

____

____

FEMALE SEXUALITY is a decoy to absorb.

MARY.CONVICTIONS.SPIRITUAL ITY.ASCETICISM.SPIRITUAL PRACTICE

SPIRITUAL DEVELOPMENT takes a person to a new higher level, opens up possibilities for the flow of subtleenergy, and the shore increases our connection with **THE DIVINE SPIRIT**, which is with us. A spiritually developed person becomes happier, more conscious, more joyful, understanding comes with the interaction with the world and universal.

Subtle energy in the context of spiritual development we receive when:

- we are starving;
- we perform breathing exercises;
- united;
- we make a vow of silence for a while;
- walk (just located) on the shore of a reservoir (sea, ocean, lake, river ...), through the mountains, just contemplate the beautiful landscapes of nature;
- we are engaged in selfless creativity;
- we praise people and note they are good qualities;
- laugh, rejoice, smile heartily;
- help someone unselfishly;
- show modesty;

- pray before a meal;
- eat foods full of vitality: natural cereals, cereals, ghee, honey, fruits, vegetables;
- sleep following our biorhythms and give the body time to relax so that the subsequent filling with life energy is comfortable for him;
- massages self-massage influences most graciously the readiness of the body to receive the subtle and powerful Divine energy of the Universe;
- we share and sacrifice our resources in goodness (smiles, attention, a conscious look of a person, care, material goods ....) with the living creatures free of charge. Resources in a sense;
- we are aware of the presence of God in everything.

Spiritual practices, meditations take place on the path of spiritual development, it's essential to realize that all these are just tools on the spiritual path.

LIFE is our main spiritual practice! The primary spiritual practice in relationships, in the streets around us! Main spiritual practice is concentration and selfless service in the world. Concentration on a person at the moment of communication, focus on what is happening around at that moment. And only is it possible to realize the intensity of what is truly necessary and essential for a person and a living being nearby and to give it to him (if there is a resource for this) through non-refundable service. How can you serve it free of charge, you ask. Gratuitous service is possible only through love, through absolute and unconscious love for all living things around us, "how is it so possible to fall in love," to fall in love, it is possible through awareness of loneliness with all living things.

If you imagine that the person who met us on the way is the same soul, like you who came to serve this world, the same as you but developed in another body, brought up by other parents, determined by another society ... it's you but in your other manifestation. What if we imagine that we are all in this world for joint service and the embodiment of an ideal Divine plan for the benefit of all living beings.

That if you perceive your neighbor not as a competitor, but as a partner, interaction with which in any of its (resource and non-resource) manifestations is necessary and important for God and the Universe. Always remember! You are not alone! God and the Universe love you in all your manifestations, with a whole set of qualities and characteristics!

It remains only for you to love yourself as God and the Universe love you!

MARY.CONVICTIONS.DIET

Add products of the following categories to the diet:		Remove products of the following categories from the diet:	
sprouted grains		citrus fruits	
wheat sprouts		beans	
nuts		roots	
fruits		meat	
vegetables		fish	
		seafood	

RECOMMENDATIONS FOR THE USE OF GERMINATED WHEAT GROWS AS ALTERNATIVES TO CASES AND BREAD

Substances that are part of the germinated wheat grains stain the immune system and provide energy to the human body. They cleanse the liver, kidneys, bladder, intestines, help relieve swelling to improve the condition of the skin and hair.

FOR THE BENEFIT

EVA. EMOTIONS.LOVE. PRACTICE

It is necessary to distinguish emotions. One has to understand is he/she angry or simply hungry; annoyed with a beloved or merely tired, happy, or surprised only then you will be able to understand what actually is going on around you.What is a reason for your worries, and react to them adequately? Also, it is essential to learn how to respond appropriately to your fears. Tears are a useful method for a body to release the tension. Disgust is a reason to refuse something you can not "digest," whether it is a tasteless dish or an unpleasant person, wherehappiness is a way to increase your energy and recharge. All of that does not in any way harm those who are around. We must learn to accept all our emotions, positive and negative, and allow yourself to express them. It is the only way to feel alive.

Write down a list of emotions that you experience. Read them out loud. What do you feel, when you speak about your emotions,explore them?

____

____

____

____

EVA. EMOTIONS.LOVE.MEDITATION

MEDITATION ACCORDING TO THE ENERGY OF ARCHETYPE EVA EMOTIONS LOVE "DISCOVERY OF THE HEART FOR UNCONDITIONAL LOVE"

TAKE A CONVENIENT BODY POSITION so that your feet touch the surface of the floor or the ground, close your eyes, CONCENTRATE BREATHING through the point of the sun.

Plexus, do three deep looseningsbreaths and exhale. Gather the focus of your attention to the point of the solar plexus, imagine how your awareness has acquired a look of a beautiful golden shiny haze,perhaps your unconscious will offer you another option, and this is wonderful,Imagine how from this golden cloud down (through both legs to the ground) to the top (through the crown chakra to the sky) pass beautiful golden channels. Two channels that pass through the legs and exit from the body through your feet, the thickness of the mother earth, and go straight down to its core. Imagine the top gold channel coming out of your body through the crown chakra and ascends high into the sky to the space of the beloved Universe.

Imagine in your mind how it penetrates through both channels into your body of benevolent energy of the

Universe, fill them with maximum and pleasure. Gather strength from three ropes down the abdomen in a place where a female uterus is located. When you feel that you are as full as possible with a stream of life-giving energy of the Universe, thank mother Earth and the higher space for filling, disconnect the channels and localize them in the same place below the abdomen where the energy is collected in the form of a golden glow.

Mentally concentrate on the golden glow and smoothly move it to your body where your heart is located, which is comfortable for you. If there are places in the body requiring healing, stop the energy in the form of a golden glow on them, and then continue to move it to the heart.

Placing a golden luminous cloud in the place of the heart, imagine how it transforms and takes the shape of a heart. It can be golden a dense heart or a luminous smoky one (the unconscious will successfully cope with this task). Imagine that this heart begins to glow in thousands of beautiful golden sun teachings that pervade your body and go outside through your body to shine and transmit love into the world and surrounding her with living things.

Continue to present yourself as the sun that shines into this world with love from the heart. After imagining that the rays smoothly transform into a golden cloud around you and envelop the space around you with a transparent haze.

Focus on your breathing and open your eyes when ready.

I recommend doing meditation in the morning before starting the day and going out into the world and carrying love.

Love people!

EVA.EMOTIONS.LOVE.DIET

ARCHETYPE EVA LOVE DIETsupplemented with products that enhance the female energy and beneficially affect the female hormonal background.

Add products of the following categories to the diet:		Remove products of the following categories from the diet:	
Vegetables		Meat	
Fruits		Eggs	
Seafood		Fish	
Beans		Fast foods products	
Whole grain breads			

RECOMMENDATIONS OF THE USE OF BEAN PRODUCTS FOR A WOMAN'S ORGANISM.

Legumes normalize the hormonal background of the female body. Legumes contain a large number of phytoestrogens than relieve the symptoms of a woman's menopause. Products of this group strengthen the heart and blood vessels due to the high potassium content. Remove toxins, improve memory and performance, indicated for diabetes contain natural antidepressant lysine, and positively affect intestinal microflora. After 45 years, women recommend that women generally remove meat and switch to legumes, which will significantly improve health indicators, maintain healthy hormonal levels, and prolong youth.

FOR THE BENEFIT

EVA.CONVICTION.LOVE.PRACTICE

Write a list that includes two categories related to your sexual life (self-perceptions, "tricks," techniques and spiritual worries). List sensation that you had at the time of sexual satisfaction. In the first column, write things that were lost. Is there something from the second column that you want to restore? What is it? What will you do for that?

SHADOW: it is not always necessary "to get up to" something unreal, sometimes it is enough to do something you have already done.

____

____

____

____

____

____

____

FEMALE SEXUALITY - is her refined expertise in here favorite subject

EVA.CONVICTION.LOVE.SPIRITUAL PRACTICE

SPIRITUAL PRACTICE FOR DISCLOSING THE ENERGY OF ARCHETYPE EVA CONVENTION.

Preparing your favorite childhood dish will open your heart to love with the help of memories and pleasant emotional experiences associated with them.

Write a letter of forgiveness selectively to someone of a kind, or refer to the type of energy in the message as a whole. Write from the heart, not from the mind. Do not analyze, but give free rein to feelings. At the end of writing a letter, thank yourself for the GREAT work done. We recommend that you include in your daily prayer practice a prayer of gratitude to your family and its individual representatives (optional). Thank God every representative of your kind, for your father and mother, for all the energy and resources that you are filled with thanks to the representatives of your kind. Call your parents, invite them to get it, organize a family dinner, and treat your family with your favorite grandmother or mother's dish from childhood.

EVA.CONVICTION. DIET WITH LOVE

Add products of the following categories to the diet:		Remove products of the following categories from the diet:	
Cooked with love beloved mom's or grandmother's dish from childhood		Coffee	
		Sweets	
		Yeast	
		Mushrooms	

RECOMMENDATIONS USE OF DAIRY FOOD FOR FEMALE ORGANISM.

Milk is one of the most valuable sources of calcium, which is absorbed by the body by more than 90%. Ayurveda doctors recommend a warm drink before bedtime.

Milk with honey. A glass of warm milk with honey has a very beneficial effect on the female body. Due to the presence of amino acids and vitamins, milk calms the nervous system and has a positive impact on sleep and improves the functioning of the endocrine, immune systems. Milk is absorbed by the action of the energy of the moon, so it is recommended to drink it after sunset.

FOR THE BENEFIT

EVA.BODY.LOVE.

Recall all the women of your kin that you have talked to. What did they say about a body, sex, men? Write these convictions down. How do they influence your life and sexuality? Rewrite them, so they would have a positive formulation.

____

____

____

____

____

____

____

____

____

____

____

____

____

____

SHADOW: it is also handy to know about the sexual relationships of your parents; about how you were conceived. You may use body therapy.

FEMALE SEXUALITY-is a light beckoning a moth.

SPIRITUAL PRACTICE. EVA. BODY.LOVE

The world around us, and our reality is a mirror image of what we carry into the world. Love is the beginning of all principles and the meaning of all meanings. Opening hearts for the love of all living things.Transformation of consciousness in the direction of perception of all living organisms with respect and equality for oneself.Understanding of all living organisms by manifestations of God in our space and time. The energy of love that we carry into the world comes back to us with the energy of appreciation of the universe and havingfilled us multiplied times, I propose to show love this week and to treat with respect all life that surrounds us (trees, flowers, plants, birds, animals, insects ...) to see not ordinary landscapes around, but to recognize the characters and emotions of all living things. For example, buy a flower (even cut) take care of flowers consciously and lovingly. Think about what water you drink it for, isn't it hot on the sunny side of your windowsill, what freshness the water that he drinks, how his leaves breathe, maybe it's time to wipe them conscious attitude with love and care! I will repeat it always and everywhere! Feed the needy and homeless on the street! Do it consciously!

Address first of all, as a person! How to a friend! Give the beggar a choice, ask a question about his desires to help him at the moment. "Do you want to eat ?" I have this, and this is, what you would like from what i have (maybe nothing so he is the same person with desires, needs, and preferences) if you are going to buy something for him, ask what he wants and accept any choice without judgment.

Radiating Love into the world, we are an example for our children! Children who have grown up in love, who have known love in all its manifestations in the future, will automatically follow your examples, without doubt, as in their happy picture of the world, you lay the concept of love from the first minutes of life! Where the energy of love grows and becomes equal, there is no place for destructive feelings and emotions.

EVA.BODY.WEEKLY DIET

Eve is the energy of love and care, delicious foods that open and bestow the emotions of the beautiful, remember, and products that carry the warm power of love.

The diet in the archetype of Eva is supplemented by a group of products that help in maintaining and improving women's health, normalizing hormonal levels, and especially useful for conceiving and bearing a child.

Add products of the following categories to the diet:		Remove products of the following categories from the diet:	
Avocado		Meat	
Salmon		Bread	
Nuts		Coffee	
Cacao		Roots	
Plants oil		Trans fats	

RECOMMENDATIONS ABOUT THE USE OF OMEGA 3 AND OMEGA 6 FOR THE FEMALE ORGANISM.

OMEGA 3 is necessary for the normal functioning of most organs of psychoemotional stability conditions. The benefits of omega 3 for the female body are well known as unsaturated acids, not only provide internal health and preserve external beauty. Unsaturated fatty acids are of the most significant value to a woman's body as, in addition to general health, they affect the reproductive function and external view.

FOR THE BENEFIT

SOFIA. BODY. PRACTICE

Affirmation is a concise, positive statement that, if repeated regularly, ensures healing and inspiring results.

Write an affirmation to achieve a positive mindset of your body in the light of your request.

____

____

____

____

When writing an affirmation, the following rules should be observed:

1. Affirmation describes the state of affairs without any problem.
2. An affirmation is formulated positively.
3. An affirmation is formulated in the first person and in the present tense.
4. Affirmation are not merely words, but they are also images behind them.
5. An affirmation has to inspire you.

FEMALE SEXUALITY - is an upturn in anticipation of filling

SOFIA.BODY. BRAIN RELAXING PRACTICE

REST FOR THE BRAIN is just as important as rest for our bodies, which subsequently leads to more productive work to create solutions for us and think more clearly. Our brain receives a continuous flow of information throughout the day (books, lectures, social networks, films, our conversations, and the people around us). When to recycle all this information ......When to sort out all the knowledge gained on the shelves, process and create from them the solution we need ... At the time of the brain's rest.

Rest for the brain is just as important as the period of loading information into it. This technique is effortless. Allow yourself at least one hour a day, it's better not to do anything for 2 hours. Protect your brain from receiving any information visually and audibly. The mind also rests in active meditation mode (running without music, preparing food not according to the recipe, all types of vigorous activity, the fulfillment of which is mechanical and does not need to be thought over process actions).

5 essential rules are defined by Kevin Bergen as a family therapist. Kevin talks about the 5 most important factors necessary for clearer thinking that arise from a competent organization rest of our brain.

These factors:

- sleep;
- meditation;
- seeing beauty;
- spiritual experience;
- information relaxation.

We recommend contemplation of nature for at least an hour a day. Concentrate on the world around you, smells, sounds. If there is no possibility of staying in nature, in any convenient place, disconnect yourself from sources and the flow of information from outside.

SOFIA.BODY. DIET

A conscious attitude to the body is the key to beauty, health, and excellent healthy physical shape. For this week, we recommend that you consider two classic essential diets to reduce and maintain body weight.

WEIGHT LOSS DIET

Add products of the following categories to the diet:		Remove products of the following categories from the diet:	
Chicken breast		Salt	
Whitefish		Spices	
Seaweed		Algae starchy	
Vegetables		Sweet fruits	
Green vegetables		Flour	
		Sweets	

WEIGHT STABILITY DIET

Add products of the following categories to the diet:		Remove products of the following categories from the diet:	
RAW SWEETS (in moderation)		FLOUR	
Vegan sweets (moderate)		Sweets	
Dried fruits		Sugar in all its	
Manifestations		Flour in all its	
Asparagus green			
Manifestations			
White asparagus			
Spinach			

RECOMMENDATIONS FOR REDUCING WEIGHT WITH THE HIGH CONTENT OF PROTEIN FOOD IN THE RATION.

A protein diet is an excellent way to lose weight without losing muscle mass and getting the nutrients you need for your body. Higher intake protein also helps strengthen bones.

RECOMMENDATIONS ON THE USE ASPARAGUS FOR WOMEN

Asparagus is especially beneficial for women. It promotes the formation of sex hormones. During menstruation, asparagus reduces bloating and pain.

At cosmetology, asparagus juice helps fight skin problems.

RECOMMENDATIONS ON THE USE OF SPINACH FOR WOMEN.

Chlorophyll fiber in the composition of spinach normalizes the intestinal tract, increase motility, and lead to natural weight loss. Delicate spinach leaves are saturated with protein, carbohydrates and fatty acids in large quantities.

FOR HEALTH WITH LOVE
FOR THE BENEFIT

SOFIA.EMOTIONS.PRACTICE

Revive your emotional sensitivity using "a cocktail of pleasures."

Make a list of everything that gives you pleasure and makes you feel sexy at the same time.

1.____

2.____

3.____

4.____

5.____

6.____

7.____

8.____

9.____

10.____

Adopt as a habit the rules of 'three pleasures a day.' Borrowed from Sysoeva.

SHADOW: adopt a rule of three revelations in your sex.

FEMALE SEXUALITY - is here self-respect, her consciousness, and her inner freedom.

SOFIA.EMOTIONS. TECHNICS

The technique of calming down and balance of emotions.

The technique is especially useful for reducing excess emotionality and increasing internal focus. Can you imagine the absolutely quiet calm of the lake?

The surface of the lake is absolutely calm, serene, smooth, reflecting the beautiful shores of the reservoir. The water of the lake is absolutely mirrored, clean, even, reflecting the blue sky, snow-white clouds, and tall trees. You just admire the smoothness of this lake, tune in to it calm and serenity. The duration of the practice is 5-10 minutes minimum at least further in accordance with your inner comfort you can describe the picture mentally listing everything that is painted on it.

SOFIA. EMOTIONS. DIET

WE RECOMMEND ADDING THE FOLLOWING GROUPS OF PRODUCTS		WE RECOMMEND TO REMOVE THE FOLLOWING GROUPS OF PRODUCTS	
Dark chocolate		Yeast	
Nuts butters		Mushrooms	
Ginseng root		Potato	
		Grains	
		Alcohol	

RECOMMENDATIONS ON THE USE OF BLACK CHOCOLATE FOR WOMEN'S ORGANISM

The benefits of black chocolate for women are extensive in their manifestations. Brain nutrition and stimulation of mental activity due to phosphorus in the composition.

Acceleration and regulation of metabolism contribute to a more effective digestive tract due to magnesium. Bone strengthening is due to black chocolate in your diet to strengthen your teeth, treat a sore throat, improve mood, relieve women's period, prolong youth, reduce production cortisol (stress hormone) ensures the presence of this magical product in the diet.

FOR THE BENEFIT

SOFIA. CONVICTION. PRACTICE

Write down all unfinished business that burdens you and takes away your sexual energy. Examine it and highlight those point, that you will finish and those that you will put aside from your life forever.

FEMALE SEXUALITY - is regular spontaneity.

SOFIA. CONVICTIONS. TECHNIQUE

TECHNIQUE FOR INTERNAL FOCUSING AND ORDERING OF EMOTIONALITY ARCHETYPE SOFIA BELIEF

Imagine that you are watching a video of today's (or yesterday) day of your life, from the side, like in a movie theater. Remember, in all the tiniest details of how your day went. How did you wake up, what did you do in the morning, how did you prepare to leave the house, how did you leave, what were small and significant an all-day event, with whom and what they talked about, which happened in the late afternoon.

SOFIA.CONVICTIONS.DIET

According to this archetype, we recommend adding "pepper" to the diet and adding "spices" to life. This simple recommendation is similar to what we clean. Any restrictions and add a spicy taste of life.

WE RECOMMEND ADDING THE FOLLOWING GROUPS OF PRODUCTS		WE RECOMMEND TO REMOVE THE FOLLOWING GROUPS OF PRODUCTS	
Black chocolate with chives		Sweets	
Dark chocolate with sea salt		Baking	
Ginger		Fried food	
Spicy spices		Animals	
Honey		Onion	
Lemon		Garlic	
FAT			

RECOMMENDATIONS ON THE USE OF GINGER AND HONEY FOR WOMEN'S ORGANISM

GINGER COMBINED WITH HONEY IS VERY FREQUENTLY USED for health purposes as these 2 components are potent antioxidants. Natural and healthy.

The remedy for the body is ginger in combination with honey. It is being used with great success to strengthen the immune system, to cure some diseases, and also to support the beauty.

FOR HEALTH WITH LOVE

FOR THE BENEFIT

LILITH.BODY.PRACTICE

Take a paper and divine a sheet of it into two parts. In the first part, write about everything you like in your body. In the second - everything you dislike. For each description, draw an imaginary character. Well, what does she fell, what does she do, what happens in your life due to that character? Do this with both characters, transforming all judgment into positive statements describing the usefulness of each feature. Nature does nothing without a purpose.

FEMALE SEXUALITY - is all that remains on you when you take your clothes off.

LILITH.BODY.TECHNIQUE

The technique to enhance pleasure this week, "breast massage."

The female breast from centuries ago is a symbol of femininity and motherhood, fertility, and prosperity.

The female breast is directly connected with the heart chakra and carries the energy of love and happiness. Female breasts are a unique manifestation of feminine nature, which endowed us with a unique opportunity to feed our children milk.

BREAST MASSAGE

Take a comfortable pose and take three deep breaths in and out with your stomach, relax. Rub your palms until they are warm, and then lay them on the chest. Send your breasts the gentle energy of your hands. Using special breast oil or a piece of tissue with gentle circular movements of the fingertips rub your chest about 3.5-4 cm from the nipples. Start from the center of the chest up and down in a circle. Repeat at least 9 times, then massage.

The entire breast, gently pressing on her tissue and rubbing in a circular motion.Pay attention to what makes you feel good, other touches, and stronger.

USE OF ESSENTIAL OILS CAN STRENGTHEN HEALING EFFECT

LILITH.BODY.DIET

ENJOY! LOVE YOURSELF! VALUE YOURSELF! TAKE
CARE OF YOURSELF! NURSE YOUR FAVORITE AND
TREAT YOURSELF AS YOUR BIGGEST VALUE.
REMOVE FROM DIET THIS WEEK FOOD WHICH IS NOT
FOR PLEASE

- fast food more than once a week
- heavy sweets more than once a week

ENJOY FINALLY FOOD WHICH ITSELF HAVE NOT
ALLOWED
ADD DURING THIS WEEK

- cardio workout sedentary
- fragrant baths
- scented candles
- incense

FAVORITES RECOMMENDATIONS

ENJOY EVERYTHING!
ENJOY EVERY PERFECT INSTANCE OF YOUR LIFE!
ENJOY THROUGH THE FEELING OF EVERYTHING
CONCERNING THE BODY, DIRECTLY, AND PORTABLE
MEANING WITH PASSION!

FOR THE BENEFIT

LILITH.EMOTIONS.PASSION.BOD Y RENTAL

The features that we dislike in others also belong to your shadow. This is something we do not allow ourselves to demonstrate. There is nothing good or bad in that, it is simply an opportunity to learn something about yourself and become more coherent. What kind of women you do not like? what do you prevent yourself from doing that they do?

____

____

____

____

____

____

____

____

FEMALE SEXUALITY-is static on the man's logic air.

MEDITATION FOR LILITH EMOTION.PASSION.

Meditation addressed to the Goddess of love, arouses sexual energy in women, makes her attractive in the eyes of men. To get rid of complexes, to make impudent, to teach to enjoy oneself and give pleasure-all, this can be done through meditation. The feminine, awakened by meditation, will become an internal fire that will never go out.

First, you need to learn how to control breathing. This is the unique technique that reveals consciousness, preparing for the next stage. You need to lie on your back, relax. It is essential to ensure that the spine is straight. First, you need to breathe in a regular rhythm, then, gradually accelerate to 50 breaths exhalation per minute. During the breathing, the chest, abdominal muscles should move. After several stages of quick breathing, you need to move on to working on intimate muscles.

On inspiration, abdominal muscles should be dragged in sharply, genital muscles should be squeezed. As you exhale, relax. You can perform the exercise for no longer than 5 minutes, be sure to relax after each approach. The second part of the exercise is also performed, but the genital muscles must be tense.

The daily of this meditation helps to know oneself, improve intimate life.

LILITH. EMOTIONS.DIET

STRENGTHEN feelings, expose emotions, heat up passion!!! This week's motto is "passion, feelings, emotions that we receive through stimulation of taste receptor."

WE RECOMMEND ADDING THE FOLLOWING GROUPS OF PRODUCTS		WE RECOMMEND TO REMOVE THE FOLLOWING GROUPS OF PRODUCTS	
COFFEE		Yeast	
Chocolate		Fizzy drinks	
Spicy spices		Fast food	
Indian cuisine		The process of taking food on	
The go		Rushing food process in a hurry	
Freshly squeezed root juices			

Pineapples			
White asparagus (strong aphrodisiac)			

RECOMMENDATIONS USE OF COFFEE FOR WOMAN'S ORGANISM

Over time, more and more work appears confirming the positive effect of coffee on the female body. Scientists have come to the conclusion that caffeine reduces body weight through a stimulating effect, accelerates metabolism, and suppresses appetite. Moderate consumption prevents the risk of illness.

Alzheimer's principal active ingredient in coffee is caffeine. It charges the body with vigor, raises tonus vessels, improves the digestive tract and other body systems.

So what is the use of coffee for women:

- IMPROVEMENT OF METABOLISM AND AS A RESULT OF DECREASE IN WEIGHT
- PREVENTION OF DEPRESSION
- IMPROVEMENT OF MEMORY, ATTENTION AND MENTAL ACTIVITY

●HELPS TO SAVE YOUTH AND A BEAUTIFUL
APPEARANCE THANKS TO ANTIOXIDANT
PROPER

FOR THE BENEFIT

LILITH. CONVICTIONS. PASSION.BODY RENTA LILITH. CONVICTIONS. PRACTICE

Did you experience situations when in the heat of the moment, having sex, you wanted to do something extraordinary but did not do that because you were afraid of the partner's reaction? How often does that occur?

Does that help you unfold completely in your sexuality?

What are you ready to do with that?

____

____

____

____

____

____

FEMALE SEXUALITY-is the balance between gentleness and audacity

LILITH.CONVICTION. TECHNICS OF PLEASURE

Today is a day of pleasure. Indulge yourself with what you have long wanted, but for some reason, did not allow yourself. Be sure to buy flowers for your beloved fill the space around you today with beauty! Fill the space around you today with love for yourself. Allow yourself all that is possible for a given period of time from the list of pleasure that has been put off for a long time. Remember that state of pleasure that will arise in the process.

Give it shape, color, what it feels like, what is the temperature. Define for this state a separate place within you. And when you feel dissatisfaction in life or not a resource state mentally get this state inside your head, it fills it with all your inner space. Then thank him for the work, thank Universe for help, thank yourself for the great job you did, thank your unconscious and mentally put your fortune back into his house inside of you.

LILITH.CONVICTION.DIET

Down with dullness! This week's experiments burst into your life at high speed!!! Experiments with the outward appearance, with the way of life, the method of thinking, and of course, the way of nutrition. We cancel the traditional food, "casual," and the usual food in the diet. We create a diet including new ones with rich tastes and flavoring products, products stimulating taste buds, and not only.

The motto of the week:

"enjoy the new and down with everything old and outdated."

WE RECOMMEND ADDING THE FOLLOWING GROUPS OF PRODUCTS		WE RECOMMEND TO REMOVE THE FOLLOWING GROUPS OF PRODUCTS	
EXPERIMENTS WITH FOOD seafood		traditional	
food (we recommend		Your standard	

oysters)			
the usual daily food			
Serve beautifully the main food priyoms during the day (preferably a week) Your standard weekly set from the food basket		sparkling	
a trip to the restaurant in a cocktail dress, stockings, and high heel shoes		carbonated	
water			
exotic fruits (we recommend fruits which are aphrodisiacs.)			
sweet drinks			

CHAMPION AMONG PRODUCTS OF THE WEEK"APHRODISIAC PRODUCTS"

Aphrodisiac products can enhance love passion, kindle desires in a chemical way. Aphrodisiac products are the very first medicinal means of enjoyment.

This is the very first apple known throughout the world at all times among all peoples to which Eve fed Adam.

Since then, the dominant group of aphrodisiac products has held a high place of honor in the gastronomic culture of the world the product "king" among the products of aphrodisiacs is "Oyster."

Oyster contains a large amount of iron and zinc, which is why they are associated with their stimulating effect. I agree that even the first glance at the "sexual" oyster brings aesthetic pleasure. Moreover, the oyster is a source of dopamine, a hormone of desire, including sexual.

FOR THE BENEFIT

TECHNIQUE FAREWELL TO ALL THE OLD AND OBSOLETE IN YOUR LIFE IN THE FULL MOON

The fool moon period is a great time to say goodbye to everything you want to leave your life. Write a letter of gratitude to all your fears, grievance, anxieties, overweight, problems, toxic relationships, all that no longer serve you well in your life. Fill each of these states mentally with resources. Think about how these conditions could help you with the good all this time. Accept them as a part of yourself and release them with gratitude.

Describe in a letter how grateful you are to them for the resources with which they are filled and ready to let them go separately from you. Compose a letter from the heart without analyzing, without thinking about the meaning of words. Dispose of the letter in any way that is most effective based on your picture of the world(burn, shine on the toilet, tear and let goun the wind.....)

DIET IN THE FULL MOON PERIOD

A DIET FOR 24 HOURS DURING THE FULL MOON PERIOD
A DIET FOR 6 DAYS DURING THE FULL MOON PERIOD

It begins on the eve of the full moon after dinner and lasts 24 hours we recommend drinking only plain water.

3 days before the full moon - in the diet only fruits and vegetables.

24 HOURS only water, freshly squeezed, and juices full moon-day.

2 days after a full diet in the diet, only fruits, and vegetables.

RECOMMENDATION FOR WOMEN DURING THEM MOON PERIOD

The main recommendation and practice for women during the menstrual period is a decrease in labor activity, a reverent attitude towards oneself, rest, and remember to pamper yourself! The menstrual period for a woman is like a well-deserved monthly rest, which will surrender even the most powerful workaholics. The UNIVERSE AND MOTHER NATURE took on the function of creating this beautiful monthly week for women to remind her of her great feminine nature, here value, her importance in this world, about the need to preserve, grow and cherish these gifts in herself.

WOMEN MOON PERIOD DIET

RECOMMENDATIONS relate to the process of menstruation and the preceding period correctly and consciously. LOVE YOUR BODY!

Body and, of course, treat yourself as much as possible! Pamper yourself as much as possible, including relaxation!

WE RECOMMEND ADDING THE FOLLOWING GROUPS OF PRODUCTS		WE RECOMMEND TO REMOVE THE FOLLOWING GROUPS OF PRODUCTS	
Milk excess		Solly	
Low-fat cheese		Smoked products	
Cottage cheese		Heavy products	
Green vegetables		Trans fats	
Broccoli			
Bananas			
Nuts			
Sunflower seeds			
Oysters			
Sweet potato			

RECOMMENDATION PRODUKT IS A SWEET POTATO. THE SWEET POTATO

IS ONE OF THE magical foods that will balance your blood sugar and love on your hormones.
